HISTORY, PERSONAL
AND POETIC

Also by Jack Maze

Scagel, R. F., R. J. Bandoni, J. R. Maze, W. B. Schofield, and J. R. Stein. *Nonvascular plants, an evolutionary survey.* Wadsworth Publishing Co., Belmont, California. 1982.

Scagel, R. F., R. J. Bandoni, J. R. Maze, W. B. Schofield, and J. R. Stein. *Plants, an evolutionary survey.* Wadsworth Publishing Co., Belmont, California. 1984.

Daniel Brooks and Jack Maze. *More Than Meets the Eye: A Poetic and Photographic Exploration of the Biologist's World* published by CreateSpace in September, 2010.

History, Personal and Poetic

Jack Maze

iUniverse, Inc.
Bloomington

History, Personal and Poetic

iUniverse books may be ordered through booksellers or by contacting:

iUniverse
1663 Liberty Drive
Bloomington, IN 47403
www.iuniverse.com
1-800-Authors (1-800-288-4677)

ISBN: 978-1-4620-2125-3 (sc)
ISBN: 978-1-4620-2126-0 (ebk)

Printed in the United States of America

iUniverse rev. date: 05/13/2011

Contents

Preface

There are two parts to this book. The first, Passages Through Time, is a collection of poems representing personal reflections on history, as captured in both human and natural events. The former include true and fictional accounts and the emotions from melancholy to gladdening. The natural happenings focus on the beauty of the surrounding world, a beauty that may counteract disheartening emotional reactions to the unavoidable challenges of life.

The second part, Guillermo, is a poetic tale of my great, great grandfather, baptized William Robert Garner in the Anglican Church of England, re-baptized Guillermo Roberto Garner in the Catholic Church in California. Some of this poem is based on a partial biography of Garner by Donald Munro Craig (see Garner, W. R. 1970. *Letters from California 1846-1847* Edited, with a sketch of the life and times of their author, by Donald Munro Craig. University of California Press, Berkeley, CA). Other parts of Guillermo rely on information unavailable to Craig as well as family legend and, of course, poetic license.

Is there a message in Guillermo, something that emerges from the words? That is for others to decide. But as I was reading about Garner, exchanging stories with relatives and working on this poem one thought continually intruded: a noteworthy life requires the intersection of two things, exceptional circumstances and a soul that can rise to meet them.

Lastly, I hope these personal reflections will offer a way to view, and accept, the inevitable. Also, perhaps more importantly, offer the reader pleasure.

These poems were produced over a 30 year period. They would not have been written, nor appear in this book, without the invaluable assistance of a large number of people, Mishtu Banerjee, Pam Curry, Dan Brooks, Cy Finnegan, Jane Parker, Kali Robson, Lee Richardson, Cathie Schorn and Paul Trejo. But the most important person was my wife, Ellie Maze.

Passages Through Time

Passages Through Time is dedicated to the memory of Bob and Carol Betker, two exceptional people who contributed to this collection with a level of wisdom, wit and humor rarely encountered.

Wreckage

These bits of metal
Scattered on the ground
Tell of a pilot,
No longer,
Homeward bound.

Autumn's Gift

Trapped in leaves
Scattered on the ground
   They wait,
      On worms,
      On microbes,
      On abrasion,
      On winter's rain,

For dissolution.

Hoping to be chosen
   By sun's energy,
   By plant roots,

To be part of spring's rebirth.

To hear
   Birds calling for a mate,
   Water flowing over rocks.

To smell
   Growing plants,
   Opening flowers.

To live once again.

Leaves' Obligation

Leaves have an obligation,
    To assure the future;
        Of the trees,
        Of the forest.

They do this under a canopy of green, comprised
    Of many hues,
    Of many textures,
    Of many shapes,

But all green.

When their obligation's been discharged

They celebrate;
    They transform their greens to brilliant hues;
        Scarlets,
        Yellows,
        Oranges.

And sharpen their contrast

With autumn's clear blue skies.

To welcome winter,
    And its renewing sleep.

Winter Buds

Cold air, morning fog,
A plant glistening in ice,
Life in suspension.

But a trade's coming.
Winter's decoration for
The aura of spring.

Ice reflecting light
Brilliantly, for the soft green
Of just opened buds.

Winter's frozen past
For future's promise and the
Smell of growing plants.

Quaking Aspen

A clear autumn sky
Would not be so blue
  Were it not
    For aspen leaves,
      Quaking yellow in the breeze.

Arbutus

Red trunks in a background of green,
Scarlet pickets in a coastal forest,
Bearing small branches loosely serpentine,
Bearing leaves which form a green crest.

Leathery leaves, green, glassy and stiff,
Hanging with margins that are finely toothed,
Bunched at twigs' ends like leafy green glyphs
And transforming light so it's softly diffused.

Clusters of flowers drooping at twig's end
Form a thin white bonnet on the tree,
Comprised of numerous small urns that lend
Uniqueness emerging as a floral symmetry.

And from these flowers, with season's flow,
Small fruits redden in the summer sun's glow.

Spring Buds

They're children of spring
Stirred when winter's chill is broken
By lengthening days,

By warm gentle rain,
By rising temperatures,
By birds singing. Once

Freed, buds begin to
Explore. Their passage is known
By the odor left

Behind as the buds
Seek new space, places where they
Can live, can survive.

The buds are agents
Negotiators between
The plant and its world

So the plant will know
If, when, how it must adjust
For its enduring.

If the plant doesn't
Survive the buds, too, are doomed.
And without the buds

Spring will not come.

Trees

The base:
    Parts, twisting and turning,
    Connections, made and broken,
    Pathways, confused and chaotic.

The crown:
    Parts separate and detached,
    Connections, branch on branch.
    Pathways leading outward to the sun.

Trees:
    A conduit for water
    Linking the earth and sky.

Dreams

In her youth, she had a private dream.
As a beautiful dancer of skill and grace
Who'd translate music to a new theme
So it would come to stand in physical space.

The clothes she'd wear would be stunning
And gently 'round her body they'd flow,
Transforming the music that's running
From the score to deep in her soul.

But the dream never came to fruition
And now she just lives day to day,
Fighting, blindly, with age's attrition
As her spirit passes into decay.

She held nothing in the dreams lieu,
With the death of the dream, she died too.

You Just Can't Understand

I can't understand why you let this happen Cyndy?
You've allowed yourself to be chained
By that incessant thumping overhead
And the scratching of an ineffectual leg
Dragging someone barely mobile to her window and back.
And those bleak and pitiful cries;
I can just see the guilt rising in your eyes.

I've told you several times before
That I've open tickets to take us far away.
We'll dance, we'll sing, we'll forget our cares.
Don't worry about the old one overhead,
I have a friend who can get her acceptable care
In a home on the other side of town.
Granted, the smell of urine that's gone stale
Is strong, but what else can you expect
From aged ones gone incontinent,
And she can hardly detect odors anymore.
Please Cyndy, say you'll leave this burdensome chore.

You know Jack, I've been looking out at the garden.
I think this year I'll plant some scarlet runner beans.
Martha finds the red flowers rather comforting
And she likes to watch the birds, fooled by the flower's red
Into thinking they have a feast of berries at hand.
Those beans, also grow quite quickly. It gives
Her something to see through a gradual change.
She can't really follow much of that stuff on TV shows
But the sparkle in the eyes of a partly frozen face
Is evidence she is aware of a small world out back.

Thank you for your offer Jack but I must decline.
I'll not explain, I've nothing more to say.
Like you said, you just can't understand.

Yesterday—Today

Yesterday:
  Matted brown vegetation,
  Wet only because of melting snow.
  A tangled mat
    Mocking life's order.

Today:
  Leaves ordered in pairs,
  Wet with morning dew,
  Shiny covering,
    Protecting flowing sap.

  And atop those leaves:
    Smaller parts,
      Different shape,
      Different color,
      Different arrangement.
        More complex,
        Following a new mathematics.

    Smaller parts possessing a magic so powerful
      It enchants insects,
      It enchants humans,
        It's a flower;

The ultimate attractor.

Buds—Listen Carefully

Listen carefully
When you walk under a tree,
Buds are telling tales.

Remembrances of:
Spring's release from winter's chill,
The constraint of drought

Brought on by summer's heat.
The pestilence from insects
Swarming over twigs.

The buds aren't telling
Tales of their own histories,
They're not old enough

To have one. They act
As poets revealing the
Truth that a tree has

Captured in its wood.
They bring it to the surface
For those willing to

Listen carefully.

Friends

How often have I sat by this grass,
    Seen shoots that have explored new places,
    Expanding its influence?

How often have I laid beneath this tree,
    In its comforting shade,
    Enveloped in the smells of early spring?

How often, when life makes little sense,
    Has your persistence
    Offered solace?

How often when day's drudgery is stifling
    Have your forms and flowers offered release?
    Have your blizzards of plumose seeds
      Carried me elsewhere
        Beyond boredom?

Plants have two purposes.
    They give scientists
      Something to study.

    They reveal to the perceptive
      The soothing beauty underlying nature.

Does either purpose take precedence?

    That I leave to others.

Penn Cove Sunset

The sky is filled with brilliant orange and red
Mirrored on clouds above and waters below,
A lavish feast of light before us spread
Through which the vivid hues weave and flow.

And interlaced in this tapestry of light,
Suffused with the glow of deep and royal purple,
Thin bands of clouds, like soaring birds in flight,
Are fused by colors into complex ripples.

With time the light becomes a thin red band
Of color so intense the mind is seared
With images that withstand the test of time
And stay secured though history intercedes.

The sun is gone, night settles over all
The sleeping cove now waits dawn's early call.

Old Woman

My marriage was one borne of desperation,
A means to a life of less privation
Than one of paternal tyranny.

A first born son gave new meaning
To a life heretofore demeaning,
A new life that went with him to sea,
Where it stays in eternity.

Now I wait on a bluff washed by western breeze.
Vainly wait and watch for his return,
So long that my human form's been spurned
In favor of an always vigilant tree
Atop that bluff, facing always towards the sea.

I'm dead, but still my spirit waits,
A spare decaying monument to faith.

Dead Tree

Perched at the bluff top
It prays to the western gods,
With limbs long deceased.

Foggy Beach

The rolling roar accents the cries of seabirds
Bound to the beach by the enveloping mist
That blankets the earth in swirling twists
As if the bottom has dropped from the sky.

And out at sea fog horns magnify
Boat's sightless probing for others which exist,
Blindly probing like sightless duellists
Carefully sensing, their world to clarify.

We walk the beach, each with private thoughts,
Silent symphonies fused to muted sound,
Of gulls and rocks, rattling in the waves.

Quieted Beach

Fog sets gently down
A gray mist muting all sound
Of the restless sea.

Fog

Fog blankets the earth like a quilt of gray
Cutting off tops of tall ridge-running trees.
And in the swales and dips stand barren sprays
Of stems suffering from winter's consequence.
The suspended water droplets soften light
To lessen contrasts in the views perceived.
A gentle change in hue, altered sight,
So different sculptured worlds are received.

In this hushed environment thin mists
Weave a complex picture of grays and greens.
A tapestry wherein colors weave and twist
To create in the depths of mind, new scenes.

Scenes that take you far beyond vision
To clearly see truth's precision.

Foggy Solitude

The gray fog muffles
Sound and mists a surface
To create solitude.

Beach Wanderer

A lone figure stalks the rocky beach
Scanning far and near for agates,
Small polished stones that catch sun's rays
Which then are reflected in sparkling light.

Though the figure stalks off alone
On a beach without a soul,
In the midst of crowds still she'd be alone,
Hearing naught but the waves gentle roll.

A lone figure wrapped in the memories of time,
Moving slowly along the flat shore
As she climbs through the paths of her history
Wrapped deep within her quiet private lore.

Though agates are the target of her mind
It is greater reason that she finds.

Beach Perceptions

The incoming tide
Soothes then heals a beach
Scarred by summer footprints.

Carol's Agates

It was foggy, cool,
    An onshore breeze was blowing.

We prepared to return Carol's agates to West Beach
    From where they'd come.

As we stepped onto the beach we heard
    Welcoming voices;
        The rattle of rocks as waves receded,
    A gull's cry,
        Offering us his beach.
All with a background
    Of wind,
    Of waves.

We tossed Carol's agates,
    Some into the sea,
    Some onto the beach,

With the hope they'd be found again
    So someone else could know
        Carol's joy of discovery.

We finished.

Then stood looking out,
    Over the beach,
    Over the ocean,

And for a second all was silent;
    The wind,
    The waves,
    The gull,

As Carol's spirit was welcomed home.

Convergences

We get a lot of news from Everett, WA,
   Compute times to Seattle,
   Construction closures on I-5,
   The Aqua Sox,
   Convergence zones north of Everett.

But this news comes not only as information.

It comes,
   Bearing her smile,
   Bearing her laugh,
   Bearing her stories,
   Bearing her eyes,
      Especially her eyes.

News from Everett, WA will never be the same.

Beach History

Footprints in the sand
Go off into winter's gray
In search of their cause.

Old Woman's Song

Another bit of gold from across the sea
Meant seemingly to ease the state
Of a life based on charity,
My loss of face, my fall into disgrace.

My life didn't start at this lowly level.
A wealthy father meant early eminence.
And on my husband, family fortune fell
To assure prolonged social significance.

But then our farm was lost to faulty plan
And my husband disappeared in shame.
The estate that was mine by birth was gone
And so till death, I live in pauper's pain.

But with the money I've been sent I'll mark my grave
So in death I'll have the status that I crave.

A Presence

Flowing through a pattern I perceive
A warm breath slowly redefines my mind
To condense like mist in cooling morning air
To weave a form I alone can see.

I can neither grasp nor recreate this form
Yet its truth is perfectly received.
I stop and try to catch this thing that guides,
That mutes the chaos which confounds the eye.

Now I can clearly hear the voice
Speaking softly, softly from beyond the page,
Speaking softly, softly from beyond the grave
Speaking softly, softly to where a claim is laid.

Ghost Town

Shells of gray and weather-beaten pine
Search for souls that no longer exist,
Faded with the passing of the mines
Deserted with the depletion of the ore.

The winds weave a mind's eye image
Forming a covert cloth which now endures
As small dust storms trying to perceive
The spirits which time has made obscure.

Windows look out onto oblivion
And only see their bleak and empty stare
Searching for life in their own skeleton
But finding only the empty desert air.

Where tumbleweeds search the empty streets
For a moment that they'll never meet.

Going Home

I grew up in a small prairie town,
    My father had worked there for a bit.
I never fit in with the rest of the kids,
    Didn't hunt,
    Didn't fish,
    Didn't play sports;
    Mostly read.

There was one place I found solace,
    Old Mrs. Water's garden.
I'd lay
    Enveloped in the sweet smell of lilac
    Protected by the iris standing guard.
Mrs. Waters would tell stories
    When she was growing up;
        Prairie springs,
        Tornadoes,
        Quiet falls,
        Winter's icy outhouse seats.

I left that rather drab little town
    Vowing never to return.

But still my travels brought me there.

I knew Mrs. Waters would be gone,
    She was frail when I left
        20 years ago.

I found the town abandoned.
    Buildings were hollow shells,
    Clothed in wood
        Weathered gray.

Vacant windows, most with broken panes
    Stared blankly at each other,
    Conveying messages devoid of meaning.

I found Mrs. Waters' house.
    It too was abandoned,
    A hollow shell of gray.

Her garden was no longer the neat place I'd remembered,
    The place that had given me so much pleasure.
      Trees unpruned for years grew uncontrolled,
    Rank grasses were everywhere.

I was standing immersed in melancholy
    When I smelled the lilacs.

I turned around
    And saw the irises.

And Mrs. Waters was again with me.

Passage

Trapped behind glass
On walls of blue and white
The past plays to empty chairs.

Company Town

Rows of houses standing stark and bleak
Looking out on dusty, curb less streets
With empty eyes that no longer seek
A world in which new images can meet.

And over all hangs a stifling pall
Settling down as clouds to earth are bound
Covering all with a gray blanketing shawl
Stifling all but dreariest of sounds.

A place where one looks out upon the world
And sees the past in the father's eyes
And in the son's sees futures unfurled.
The highest point is the day you die.

A town by a single mill embraced
A place where the future is debased.

Virg

Her paintings caught the island's ambiance,
Abandoned barns and false front village stores,
Distorted trees at the bounds of subsistence,
Cabins lining clam encrusted shores.

From her subtly complex illustrations,
One can see the life below veneer;
Spirits stand outstretched in isolation,
Histories telling tales for all to hear.

Far below the surface of a view
There lies in wait a new observance theme,
A thread weaving through the common hue
Constructing sights heretofore unseen.

She could point out new worlds to be sought
Because she knew how meaning could be caught.

La Conner, Washington

Pilings lining the pale green waters
Underlie reds, whites, and grays marking town.
And mansions of rich village fathers
Look down on the rest from low hills.

Anchored there are boats of many kinds
Thin-hulled, sailing ships with tall masts,
Motor cruisers, clean but less sleekly lined,
Fishing boats conveying tales of storm tossed trips.

And rusty derelicts with near sunk hulls
Tell silent tales of bygone journeys
Through heavy seas and peaceful lulls
To return again, to harbor's lee.

I sit on a hill as this world unfurls,
A reverie now broken by blue jay scold.

The Room

The blue walls
  bear
    glass trapped
      private and public histories.

Histories
  studied
    by vacant chairs
      seeking a tie to a common past.

A past
  constructed
    out of bits,
      isolated moments tied together with time,
  to define unique events
    as hard and clear
    as bits of glacial ice.

But glacial ice
  will melt
    and like the past
    never exist again;

      except

in dreams of empty chairs
  staring at frozen bits of time.

Summer Dawn

The breeze carries the smell of oaks and grass
From hills down to the land below
A gentle smell that wakens with each pass
The sleeping land and starts the daily flow.

Dawn's eastern glow outlines the trees in light
And sets them off, brilliant against the sky,
Candles that mark the passing of the night,
The shadow laden time that pacifies.

The quiet of the dawn is softly broken
By the morning breeze rustling summer leaves
And movement of animals just woken
As they rise and shake off sleep's debris.

The sun climbs high in the summer sky
Life moves to shade to hear heat's lullaby.

Leaves

Those leaves,
　　They're pretty simple,
　　　　Earth,
　　　　Air,
　　　　Fire,
　　　　　　OK sunshine,
　　　　Water.

But they're all different you say.

Yup, they are.

And I could tell you how're they're made.
　　　Chemicals reacting,
　　　Cells dividing,
　　　Cells growing,
　　　Cells maturing.

And knowing all this, could I make a leaf?

Nope, not smart enough.

Homecoming

I drove up to the gate, once led onto the grounds
   Of Santa Anita School,
      Just southeast of Tres Pinos
     In the oak woodland,
        California's Inner Coast Ranges.

The fence was still there,
   But most was gone.
     The buildings,
     The basketball goal posts,
     The teeter totter,
     The volley ball nets.
   I could recognize where some things had been.
     The large white oaks we used for volley ball posts.
     The even larger live oak that shaded the teeter totter.

The rest all gone.

I thought back 65 years when I'd first arrived.
   It wasn't my choice.
   My mother had been hired to teach there,
     In a one-room school
     Just south of nowhere.

When we first arrived my eye was caught by the birds.
   They had an odd way of flying.
     Flap a few beats then glide with folded wings,
       Undulating through the air.
   The birds were pretty,
     Black and white with some red on the head.
   The call was a raucous laugh
     Like they were making fun of me.
I asked what they were; woodpeckers my mother said.

The school building wasn't much,
   White-washed wood of vertical slats
  And looked like it'd been strafed.
     The fate of a wooden building in woodpecker country.

At the back of the school yard, on either side
   Were the outhouses;
     Boys on one,
     Girls on the other.
       Oddly, the outhouses lacked bird-pecked holes.
      Maybe woodpeckers do have taste.
They were no longer functional.
  Indoor toilets had been put in the year before.

There was no electricity.
   During the rare event of rain in a California winter
     It was considered too dark for school work.
    We'd fire up the Coleman lanterns
      And just have fun
        Released from the drudgery of school.

Like all school rooms, it was noisy.
   There was the normal by-product of education,
     Talking,
     Reading,
     Explaining.
But at Santa Anita there was more;
     The occasional drumming of woodpeckers on the school walls,
     The rattling of debris hitting the floor
       When a woodpecker breached the walls.

We did have a phone,
   Part of a party line.
  We knew when we were called
    We had our own signal,
      A distinctive mix of long and short rings.
  We were rarely called but could listen in to others on the party line.

Wasn't considered *de rigueur*
And was boring to boot.

The school was in the midst of a hay field
Where we could, in late spring, watch
The mowing, raking and baling of hay.

But most interesting was a little draw
Just behind the school.
In the spring my sister and I would wander there,
Lie under the slender-trunked and small blue oaks on a carpet of
Lupine,
Owl's clover,
Indian paint brush,
Chinese houses,
Grasses.
And luxuriate in the smell of a California spring.
Fresh,
Cleansing,
Invigorating.
It was years before I realized that
Was the smell of plants growing.

The next year the old building was torn down.
The new building was modern;
Electricity,
Fancy fluorescent lights,
A kitchen where we cooked hot lunches,
A movie projector.

We were impressed with the new.
All fancy,
All up-to-date,
But we were still on that party line.

But now as I stood outside that gate
Immersed in the past
Memories of the new building faded away

Leaving
That old hole-riddled structure,
The raucous calls of woodpeckers,
Their undulating flight,
Their pounding on walls.
All carried on the smell
Of a California spring.

Harold's Cap—Bob's Jacket

Harold's cap,
   "Genuine Antique Person,"
     "Been there,
     Done that,
     Can't remember it."

Bob's jacket,
   Faded blue plaid,
     Well worn wool,
     Warm,
     Comforting.

It wasn't a bad decision
   Going out in
     Harold's cap,
     Bob's jacket,
It just had effects.
   They were odd,
   But should have been predicted.

I was barely out of the house
   When Vancouver's tree-lined streets
     Were transformed.

I was dressed in waders,
   Knee deep in Penn Cove water,
   Covered with slime,
   Dumping smelt out of a seine,
   Dumping the odd salmon out of the net;
     Didn't want to,
     Law demanded it.

I stepped off a curb,
   And reel two started.

We were on Harold's front porch
   Holding tumblers of Old Fitzgerald
      Diluted only with melting ice.
   Gazing out at a Penn Cove sunset
      Filtered through the gray smoke of Dutch Master's cigars.

Another curb,
   Reel three.

We're at the Sea House on Penn Cove
   Stringing lights so clams can be dug
      On a real low tide,
         That happens to come on a midnight
            In December.
   All of us carrying a significant load
      Of Old Grand Dad.

Another curb,
   Reel four.

In the Tyee.
      For years smoking had been banned.
      Wouldn't know it though.
         Walls long steeped in cigarette smoke
         Released its stale, characteristic odor;
         Oddly welcoming.

Laughter ricochets off the walls.
   The floor was thickly littered
      In creative expositions of events
         Recent past,
         Far past,
         Imagined.
Weren't lies though.
   Lies are malicious.

A molecule of malicious would die a lonely death
In the Tyee.

Another curb,
Reel five.

I'm on the *Island Commander,*
A tug,
Hauled a load up to Attu in WW II.
We're off Attu,
Going in tight circles,
For four days.
With a destroyer going in wider circles
For four days;
Whoever said odd-ball security started with 9/11
Don't know no history.

I returned home,
Not sure where I'd been,
Not sure where my mind was.
But that's no matter.
It's beyond the age of consent.

Shadows

Why are you back there
   In the shadows
   Hidden from bright light?

We're the same,
   Furrowed,
     Me by time,
     You by history.

There's no reason for shame.

We share with all,
   The winners,
   The losers,
   The also rans,
   The ne'er do wells.

And with them we also share
   Stories beyond imagination,
   Events unbelievable,
     After the fact.

Come join me in the light.

I've got some killer stories to tell you.

Engine 89

We were taking the grandkids to Bellingham,
    Up I-5.
We'd pulled into a rest stop,
        Rested,
        Were about to leave.

I was moving onto the freeway when Rory said "Look Grandpa!"

I looked.

Coming up in the right lane was an old fire truck,
    Must have been 60, 70 years old,
    Giving its all,
        Red light on,
        Siren wailing.

I pulled aside to let it pass.

I hesitated a bit,

Then saw the damndest thing.

Every vehicle on the freeway,
    Cars, pick-ups, 18 wheelers,
    Could have out run that old fire truck.
Yet as each became aware of it
    They peeled off to the right
    And stopped,

        Actually stopped,

    Leaving the road to it alone.

As I saw it go over a rise,
   It was the sole vehicle on that freeway.

Rory asked where it was going.
   Had to admit I didn't know.

That evening watching the TV news saw a story.

There'd been a bad fire south of Bellingham.
   It was threatening to get away.

A request was made for more pumper help.

All that was available was an ancient fire truck, Engine 89,
   Restored and maintained by the fire fighters in Mount Vernon.

The call went out.
The old truck responded.

There was more to the story
   Details I didn`t follow
   But it was obvious
      Were it not for the water pumped by Engine 89
      There'd been big problems.

I turned the TV off and sat thinking.

I know inanimate things don't have thoughts, feelings
   But I had no trouble
      Imagining that old truck back in the fire house,
      Being looked after by proud and loving hands,
Recalling
   The satisfaction
      That comes from making a difference.

Old Boat

We were in Anacortes, Washington,
    At the W. T. Preston,
        An old snag boat
            Used to clear shipping channels.

    Retired in 1981,
        Now a U. S. Historic Site.

The old ship was beached on a berm of sand, pretty much intact.

    The crew's quarters,

    The galley,
        With its stove that could fry three dozen eggs at one time,

    The equipment,
        Steam engines to drive the paddle wheel, gears and winches,

    The station from which the engineer ran the ship,

    The boom used to haul snags,

    The boom man's seat,
        Behind a forest of levers.

The wheel house.

    Among the wheel and speaking tubes
        Was a rope attached to a bell.

I was told I could ring the bell.
    I did.

The sound wasn't much, between a clang and a bong.
   Not very melodic.

I rang the bell,
   Again and again.

With each peal,
   The tone became more melodic.

With each peal,
   I felt movement in the air.

With each peal,
   I sensed scurrying feet.

With each peal,
   I heard the muted sound of orders and shouts.

With each peal,
   Equipment clanked and rattled.

With each peal,
   Snags lifted again,
      Dripping mud and water.

With each peal
   The W. T. Preston was
      Once again

      Alive.

The Queen of the North

MAY DAY, MAY DAY, MAY DAY!
THIS IS THE *QUEEN OF THE NORTH*!
WE'VE RUN INTO GIL ISLAND!
   WE'RE TAKING ON WATER!
   WE'RE SINKING!
   WE'RE ABANDONING SHIP!
MAY DAY, MAY DAY, MAY DAY!

Thank God we got on a life boat Charlie.
   But it's cold, windy, rainy, in the middle of the night.
   The baby's terrified,
      I am too,
      Where are we?
      How can the Coast Guard ever find us?
Oh Charlie, I'm so scared.

Charlie, did you just hear something?
   Sounded like a motor boat.

Charlie, Charlie, look,
   There to the east,
   It's a small boat coming this way.

And look Charlie, there's more, and more.

Here's one coming up to us.
   Pass up the baby Charlie.

Thank God you're here.
   Where are you from?

Hartley Bay ma'am, an Indian fishing village just up that channel.

There's so many boats I see.

We've got lots of boats,
  All are here with The Queen.

Where are you taking us?

Our community center ma'am.
  You'll get hot food,
  Something to drink,
  Dry clothes.

Here's a blanket for your baby. He looks like he's cold.

Hang on ma'am, we're off.

Waiting Patiently

The town abandoned its existence while I was away.

Once there was life,
   Comings and goings,
   Trade and talk,
   Shared,
      Coffee and stories.

No more.

Echoes are there,
   But echoes only mimic.
      If there's nothing to mimic
         Echoes are as empty as abandoned buildings.

I missed this town and I'm patient

So I'll just wait for the people to come back.

Hannah's Fork

What century is it from?
  20th,
  19th,
  Maybe even 18th?

With prongs of iron so soft
  They bend on anything firmer than
    Oatmeal lumps,
    Boiled potatoes,
    Pabulum,
  And so require continual readjustment.

It can flip bacon or meat with facility,
  Everywhere but into your mouth.

The handle is thick wood giving a balance
  Comforting to the hand.

A comfort enhanced
  By Hannah's spirit,
    Flowing as an inspiration.
    An inspiration for happiness,
      A smiling face in a sea of seriousness.

I never knew Hannah.

But I miss her.

Suburban Development

There was a tree where I'd lay beneath the sun
And track its path through partially lidded eyes,
Listening to the lark's melodic song
Composing dreams from a springtime sky.

I took a trip to find that tree once more,
And hear the songs and smell spring sweetened air,
To return to times that I'd known before,
To days when I was innocent of care.

But the tree and singing birds were gone,
My resting place was cased in gray concrete,
The thickened air bore development's din,
Emitted from the smog enveloped streets.

I turned my back and slowly walked away,
The tree, the birds, my youth; all buried today.

An Old Man

An old man died the other day,
Think of where he's been;

    From a foot path wandering through a field,
    To a freeway's concrete base;

    From cattle grazing on green grass,
    To a town's suburban spread;

    From horses plodding homeward bound,
    To a jet plane overhead;

    From hoof prints on a wagon road,
    To foot prints on the moon.

An old man died the other day.

    Shed not a tear.

    Shed not a tear.

The Funeral

A distant kin of mine had died
In a small town where I happened to be.
I thought I should attend his funeral
Though he wasn't that well known to me.

It was easy, finding the mortuary,
A large white building, Spanish style,
With grass and palms and flowers.
I went in to find the rows of church-like pews
Lined with solemn faces and quiet voices,
And the occasional hanky touched to the corner of an eye.
And there was that cheerless organ music
That could sadden almost any tune.

I asked if there was a family room
And was directed to the front, on the right.
En route I stopped to see the recently departed,
An old man lying in a coffin covered with a floral spray.
His clothes weren't funeral standard,
A leisure suit, a patterned shirt, a bolo tie.

I turned to join the family mourners,
Taking a seat in the back of that room,
Engulfed in the ritualistic sorrow
That a funeral extracts from almost everyone.
As I sat absorbed in melancholy I gradually became aware,
The dismal funeral music could scarce be heard.
I glanced around in quizzical attention;
Few, if any, were sad or crying.
Most were in animated conversation,
Some were laughing, others telling stories
Starting with "I remember," "That reminds me,"
Or, "Remember when."

Two old ladies were talking,
One, the older and obviously blind, was saying
How he used to hate it when his sisters called him Teddy.
I was asked if I had seen the random scattering
Of fact and fiction in the newspaper account of his death,
And then was told that he was the source of most of it.

The rites began and the babble died away
As each dropped into a private reverie,
Still with few, if any, tears.

At services end, I declined an invitation
To join the family in a planned sit-down reception.
A family chore had been done
And responsibilities awaited me,
A long drive away,
In another small town south of here.

Life's Desires

What are life's desires?
Joy, happiness, success?

Perhaps.

But these do not come in isolation.

Joy's companion is despair;
As success and failure alternate,
So too do happiness and distress.

The goal of life is not a single state,
That soon will change,
But a serenity that balances
Elation's high
And depression's low,

CONTENTMENT.

My contentment has but a single source.
It comes from you.

You,

Who,

Shares my joy so it's enhanced,
Dilutes my distress so it's subdued,
Commutes my failures into practice for
Future success.

You, who defines life's desires.

Guillermo

uillermo is dedicated to the memory of my father, Theodore Francis "Dud" Maze. It was through him I gained an appreciation for family history as revealed in tales. And it was from him I also learned the value of never letting facts get in the way of a true story.

Guillermo

What you are about to read is a story, briefly told,
Of one man, of a life terminated before its years,
Of a life of culture, of rejection, of success,
Of politics, of sexual excess; a life beyond prediction.

Departure

Will I ever sail into this port again
And feel my eyes overflow with tears of joy
Spilling onto this water-roughened rail?
Will my final vision be what's before me now,
A receding port hidden by the bitterness I feel
At being cast aside by a father for a silly act?
Was I the first to scale the stone walls of that school?
Was I the only lad to ever speak out of turn?
Was I the only lad to nail a clerk's shoes to the floor?
Did those acts of animated innocence deserve this banishment
To a ship going off to gather oil to light accountant's desks,
Or fish bones to halt the spread of portly matrons,
Or enhance the form of women seeking marriage
To men who can hardly look beyond a wiggling rear
Enhanced by tightened waist and bouncing bustle.

I stand, immobilized by loneliness on a rocking ship
Looking to a future of locations remote and most unsure.
The men around me are not like those I've known,
A lot with experience, no doubt, but many incapable
Of reading or seeing value in things beyond a beer or tart
Who uses her body to tease money from a sailor's purse.
How can I talk with them? I've known only school
And the advantages of a mother's royal connections.

How could my father feel so mortified he'd banish me
To a life of ship-centered despair and danger?
I still can see my mother's tear-filled eyes
And hear her fruitless pleas uttered on my behalf.

He's your son, a boy who's yet to shave.
One who's frivolity has led him astray
And into childish pranks of immaturity.

> I beseech you to reconsider your decision,
> One so dire I can scarce believe its character.
> All he's done is show the flaws of youth.
> He's not harmed anyone. Why should he be sent away
> To a world marked by cruelty and danger?
> The world of whaling ships is one where survival is
> Often but a matter of chance and blind luck.
> He'll learn a trade, it's true,
> But is the gain congruent with the price
> He'll have to pay in pain and loneliness?

When she saw my father would remain unmoved by her words
She tried her best at an act of brave confidence
That I would ultimately benefit from my father's decision.

> William, you know I hold you in the highest esteem.
> What you now must face will be difficult indeed.
> But remember you are blessed with charm and ability.
> And soon you'll transform your current dreaded state
> Into one that will serve you and your father well.
> Be brave my son. I'll see you when you've returned
> Full of stories and grown into a man.

I still can see her gentle eyes and feel her final touch.
So different from the faces of the men with whom I stand
So different from the roughened rail beneath my hand.

Life As A Whaler

I've now become accustomed to life on board the ship
And the continual roll from the wind and waves
And the whistle as the rigging intercepts the wind.
My education before being shanghaied and sent away
Has stood me in good stead; I've become an officer
And sleep in a bunk instead of a fo'cs'le hammock
That sways as each wave's crest and trough pass underneath.
Nor must I face the frail boats used in chasing whales,
Nor fear the thrashing tail of these great beasts
As they seek revenge on those who've caused pain.
But, like all the crew, I must live with the stench
Produced by blubber being rendered into oil
And brave decks slippery with blood pouring from leviathans
As they're turned into a cargo
One that will fetch a handsome price at home
And turned into profits to be divided,
Each man to his due.

And an officer can have first call at the women,
Whose only crime was poverty or being Irish born,
Being transported to Australia's distant shore.
Carrying a human cargo may not appeal to everyone
But it means we have a cargo when outward bound.
This human payload is a source of money for misers,
The backers for our trip who want an even greater profit.
To them there is no difference between human lives
Or bone and oil, they're conduits to enhance their coffers.
And should their dreams be visited by spirits
Of those whose misery enhanced their wealth
A Sunday in church, and a generous offering, is a salve
For the righteous wrath of the Anglican God
Who knows that England's power rests in the hands
Of merchants who can only distinguish profit from loss.

These lonely and desperate lasses, especially the comely,
Prefer an officer's company to that of uncouth seaman
Whose idea of charm is restricted to baring himself
In preparation for the most brutal and efficient mating.
My good looks and gentility make me a favorite of the girls
Many who likely are incubating little Garners when
Deposited at last on Oz's arid shores after a voyage
Made longer than necessary by entertaining freight.
I sometimes wonder if I'll see them or my children again.
But such thoughts mustn't interfere with my carnal desires.
These girls differ from any one of London's common tarts
Only in where they ply their trade and their ultimate goal;
They want not so much my money but my good name and the
Prestige of my obvious breeding and officer status.
Perhaps it's good I'll not see them or their bastards again.
A flock of unwanted heirs can bring dishonor or inhibit
The pursuit of a successful businessman's life.

Fateful Voyage

I had a premonition about this trip
Even as we sailed down a tranquil Thames.
It started during a refit, cheaply done,
When I saw only the rottenest of strakes
Replaced by wood unfit for a vessel of this size.
The food we carry in our stores
Is even worse than the feed of prisoners
When the dregs of English society
Were banished to the Empire's distant shores.

My initial fears did come to pass
With a crew half-poisoned by rotten food
And water barely fit to drink.
Any compassion in our Captain's heart
Cannot penetrate beyond his avarice and panic
As we search in vain for whales
To turn into the profits that bring glee
To the money-hungry backers of this trip.
The greed that drives our captain's frenzy
Is unshared by men so weak they scarce can stand
Or row a boat or man the lines
That keep us on our course or save us
From breaching in a trough.
I've tried to tell the captain
That both ship and crew are in dire straits
Because the food we eat and water that we drink
Poisons two times for any bit of nourishment.

But at last the captain was convinced
That the peril we face, because a scurvy-wracked crew
Cannot react to any command either that of officer's
Or their own experience, places both this voyage
And his life in jeopardy. So he's decided.

Acting as if he is a man of mercy,
That we must make a port of call,
Hawaii or San Francisco; we're denied Japan
Since a visit there invites a term in jail.

We arrived on California's shore, in hilly Yerba Buena
Where our bodies could be strengthened
And our spirits renewed by the ministration of women
Who wait on each ship's landing.
We had two weeks on shore, two weeks where our senses
Weren't fouled by food or water
Or our captain's frenzied greed.
But the man lacked the patience
To let our minds and bodies truly mend,
And driven by dreams of profits set sail again
But now with a crew rife with discontent
At being jerked from the pleasures of a western Sodom.

As we cleared the Golden Gate and set a southern course
The crew became ever restless
With constantly voiced complaints
And sluggish response to officer's commands.

Their insolence was resentment borne
When half returned to health, they were drug back
To the hell of a ship ill-suited to pursue its goal again.
We were but a few days out of the sheltered bay
When my cabin was visited by some crew
Well armed and calling for a mutiny.
Their looks of wild desperation
And the memories of a scurvied crew
In a futile chase of the profits
Would override an officer's ship-centered loyalty.
It was a heinous crime they proposed
One that if we failed would assure our deaths
Should England's shores be touched again.
But these desperate men I faced were confident
The crew was with them to a man

And once the captain was confronted with a united stand
His only choice was to capitulate to save his ship and life.
There men weren't a vengeful lot,
All they wanted was an opportunity
To foresee a future unburdened by the recent past.
Their plans beyond displacement of the captain were vague;
To stay on California's friendly shores
And live the hash-like dreams offered
By San Francisco's friendly whores.
They were unaware, or perhaps didn't care,
That California's a foreign land
And may not welcome them as victims
Escaping the tyranny of those who captain ships.
But their innocence of political reality
Was evidence of a misunderstanding far more dire.
The backing of the crew on which they hoped
Vanished leaving the mob that faced the captain
A puny one indeed, a few crew and me.

The fate that we ultimately faced
As failed and captured mutineers
Was determined by the self-same acts that brought us here.
The captain's greed would not allow him to take the time
To hang us on the spot or clap us in irons
So we could be delivered to England's cruel law of the sea
From which it is decreed that, as captured mutineers,
We must stretch good English hemp.
No, the captain, with words of pompous hypocrisy,
Declared he would pass the nature of our fate
To that peaceful foreign shore sitting just to port.
So we were bound and manacled in English iron
And rowed ashore by one of the gloating cowards
Who had abandoned us in the face of English authority.

Santa Barbara

This building has an odd but pleasing look
Low and washed in white with red curved tile roof,
And walls so thick the room's secure from summer's heat,
Which, without San Francisco's cooling fog, beats
Ceaselessly down on a land parched and brown with
Only scattered oaks for shade.

I've been arrested, barely touched the shore
Before I was faced by weapon-bearing troops,
Straight from a poorly produced London comic opera.
Couldn't understand a word they said but still knew
I was to follow them to this official post.

At least the uniformed dark-skinned man before me
Has a smattering of English though he's barely literate.
And the girls on the street were truly pleasing to see
With dark tinged hair and eyes; and breasts as well I'll bet
Beneath those clothes that cover but don't confine.

As I stand here, freed at last from "The King's good iron"
And trying to answer questions asked in broken English,
I can't forget the smugness of that disgusting boor
Who manned the oars when I was brought ashore.

Billie Me Boy

That's the King's good iron you feel on your wrists,
    Billie me boy.
That's not some metal trinket given after a tryst,
    Billie me boy,
Given by some young lass captivated by your blonde charm,
    Billie me boy.
No me lad, the King's good iron will assure that no more,
    Billie me boy,
Will you play loose with the lasses we've all got eyes for,
    Billie me boy,

There's no broad river of your youth on yon shore,
    Billie me boy,
Wandering through the streets of pubs and whores,
    Billie me boy,
Where you played fast and easy with the pick of the lot,
    Billie me boy.

There's no deep oak woods where you used to play,
    Billie me boy.
There's only the dry hills where you now must stay,
    Billie me boy,

See those rounded hills that rise beyond the shore,
    Billie me boy?
Don't that covering of brush remind you of that lass,
    Billie me boy,
With only her chemise covering her gentle curves,
    Billie me boy,
The one who left my arms when you winked your eye,
    Billie me boy?

You're going to find they don't speak your tongue here,

Billie me boy,
Your fancy learning and imagination ain't no good there,
    Billie me boy.
You're being cast ashore, a foreigner breathing foreign air,
    Billie me boy.
You're doomed, me lad, you'll not live out your time,
    Billie me boy,
In the ship's wager, I say you're dead by forty-nine,
    Billie me boy,

Dead by forty-nine, that's not to be my destiny.
I've not survived these many years on a restless sea
By being dim-witted or slow. And the man I now face
Seems unconcerned about my future in this place.
It should take but a few words borne from my wits
Before I'm freed to start a life anew and make my way
While sampling freely of the charms of the dusky beauties that
I've seen along these streets. It should be but
A brief time until my intuition leads me to understand
Their speech and my loneliness will end and a future
Will be mine to make, one so secure to make the silly wagers
Of ignorant whalers the mockery that settles on fools.

California Dreaming

I've satisfied the laws of this strange land
And am free to move as I please.
The language has come to me with surprising ease
I guess that's because it's all I hear.

The continuous roll of the ship
Has been replaced by the gentle sway
Of a horse as moving along
With little attention from me.

The ocean, ever moving,
Now calm, now with waves
That tower over a ship
Or flood its decks from rail to rail
Has been switched for rolling hills and valleys,
Not as dynamic as the sea
But presenting as many different views
As a winding road reveals
Worlds not seen before.
And the spring green of grass coated hills
With flecks of blue and yellow and purple
Is something denied an ocean traveler.

No longer do I endure
The constant whistle of wind harassed rigging
And the creak of ribs and planking
As they flex over each passing wave.
Now I hear naught but rustling grass
Or the octave defying trill of the lark
As each dawn is welcomed.

No longer does the putrid smell of rotten food
Or a whale being rendered into oil

Pervade each passing day and saturate my clothes
Making the foul stench a part of me.
Now it's only plants that fill the air
With flowers' sweetness or the subtle freshness
Of plants imbuing the air with a celebration of life.

No longer is my skin assailed by unimpeded sun
Bearing down with persistence from equatorial skies.
Now oak trees offer a gentle shade
Where, when tired, I can lay
And listen to and watch and smell
A delightful world go by.

Each day starts with uncertainty
As where or what I'll eat or sleep that night.
But the weather's not so hot
By day nor cold by night
That there should be concern for lodging.
And the people spread thinly over the land
Are never more than a day's ride apart
And generous and friendly to a fault
With always open arms to who should wander by
Even a tall blonde Englishman
Whose Spanish skills are still in need of aid.
And the girls, young and dark with penetrating eyes
But watched, oh so closely watched.

I don't live a parasite's existence
Only taking as I go ranch to ranch.
I've skills to offer, carpentry or even keeping books,
If any one showed much concern
With the flow of commerce,
Or money was available to chart the flow
Of hides or wheat or tallow
Generated by the land
With hardly any interference from a human hand.

And the parties where I've been

71

Watching bodies twirling
In a kaleidoscope of colors
Dancing far far into the night
With a frenzy that pales the rising sun.
And natives so adept on a horse
You cannot tell where the rider ends
And the horse begins.
And with ropes of braided rawhide
So skilled they can subdue most any beast
From bull to raging bear.
It's a treat to watch them at this sport
A graceful dance between antagonists
Where horses respond to the riders' subtle commands
Given by shifts in weight or gentle touch with rein or knee
To avoid their target's wild thrusts.

The pleasures of this land are seductive
With charms rivalling those of women I've met
In London's bawdy houses or the holds of convict ships.

    They offer satisfaction, like a maiden's lips
    They offer gratification, like a maidens supple body.

But the charms are just as fleeting.

And a man who wants to leave a mark
Cannot dedicate his life to wanton desires
Be they from the land or from a woman.
It's been fun; my mind's refreshed.
It's time to start a new directed life
It's time to abandon the goal of simple pleasures,
To leave my mark by accumulating land and wealth;
It should be easy.
The land's forgiving and the people with few ambitions
Beyond a fandango, or fiesta, or producing children.

And the dearth of names they chose for the young.
Were Josefa, Maria or Francisca denied for girls

Or Joseph, Manual or Jesus denied for boys
The young would be responding to the likes of Girl,
Boy, Brother, Sister.
Be that as it may, the commonness of given names
Is solved by nicknames that abound.
I've been labelled as Long Legs.

Conversion

How many times have I come this way
Riding slowly towards those rounded hills
Clothed with grass and scattered oaks and patches
Of gray chemise and glossy poison oak?

How many times have I come this way
Bouyed by anticipation of seeing once again
The Butrons, Manuel and Rita, and their dark-skinned daughters,
At home in Natividad.

    The feisty and outspoken Maria,
    Young and angular;

    The older gentler Josefa
    With the rounded curves of a mature woman
    Surrogate mother to her many younger sibs.

But this time it's not the pleasures of Natividad I seek
Instead the road that leads over the Gabilans
To San Juan Bautista, a priest
And submission to a strange religion.
If I want to be part of this land, to marry
Or engage in business that is more than simple barter
I must forsake my Anglican past
And swear allegiance to distant Rome.
And an obscure old man of such authority
That his agents dictate who will or will not
Enjoy the benefits of a full and fruitful life.

But the price is small when you consider the prize,
A land waiting for someone who knows the ways of business
In order to garner the riches held within the land.

Swearing to follow the one who calls himself
The Vicar of Christ also allows entry into local society,
So by a carefully planned marriage
My business efforts can be aided
Through ties to what passes for local aristocracy.

There are other women available, both Indian and White,
And the Church cares little about who they marry.
But those families can offer only a strong back.
They haven't access to the money or influence
Necessary to generate a kingdom defined by wealth.

So now I go to kneel before a man
To swear undying allegiance to the Holy Catholic Church.
But as I utter these words of supplication
My mind will be calculating profits
And contemplating the joys of marriage.

Marriage

Now is the time when I shall take a wife
From among the offerings harbored at Natividad.
I see two choices from among Manuel's maidens.
The gentle Josefa with her curves softened by maturity,
The spirited Maria with her sharp tongue and quick wit
Whose youthful body has grown into a woman's
Fully capable, and anxious, to bear my children.
It matters not which one I chose
To realize my goals and ambitions,
They're both Butrons, aristocracy of the land
And heirs to the wealth presented by Natividad.
Gentle Josefa would offer solace from a busy day
And truly loves children, even not her own.
But she's beyond marrying age, her best years being wasted
In looking after the stream of children
Generated by Manuel and Rita's love.

So it is by default that I'm to wed Maria.
She won't be a dutiful or properly submissive wife.
But life with her will be a challenge
And hopefully the joys of the marriage bed
Will help to salve the damage delivered
By her sharp and acid tongue.

So now I stand beside my bride to be,
A girl of only 18 years, dressed in virgin white.
Here I stand, a man of more than 18 years.
Unqualified, indeed, for cloth of virgin white.
Soon formalities will end and our union will be blessed.
Soon the music will mark the paranga's start
And the passion of the dances will foretell
The pleasures I anticipate on this nuptial night.

Josefa and Santos

My marriage is not the delight I boded by my wedding night.
The spirited Maria has given me children
But she's morphed into a shrew, as shrill and hard
As many of the men I knew on whaling ships.
With each passing day of her sharp and cutting comments
Drive me to greater and greater distraction.
And with each attack I find solace in the company of Josefa,
Her gentle sister with the maturity and soft body of a woman
Desirable for her sympathy and with the love of children
I'd seen so long ago. I find myself more and more excited
By her presence, sitting quietly by me, listening to my
Lament and gently touching my arm. I find my will to resist
Her charms and the lure of her arms dissipating and I am
Consumed by passion, passion that will soon be consummated
With a night of forbidden love as my resolve to remain
Faithful to Maria is eroded by her continual criticism
And her denial of the pleasures of the marriage bed.

Now the daliance with Josefa is over
But still she clings to me as if my act
Was one spurred on by other than casual carnal delight.
And martial frustrations.

So now I seek deliverance from the shrill Maria elsewhere
To the house of a woman living the life of single loneliness
One who'd gladly welcome the experience I've gained
At sea, in bawdy houses, not in Natividad.
And the company of a man with fair countenance
And a generous bank account.
But that bitch, that ungrateful bitch
Had demanded that I be hers and hers alone.
I went into her house expecting to embrace a woman
Soft and warm and willing.

And then she said I must promise to divorce Maria
Before her favors would be bestowed on me.
I'll allow no woman to tell me what to do.
I'll tolerate no woman denying me my delights.
Perhaps I shouldn't have wrecked her house
But still it's what her likes deserve.

Now I face the prospect of divorce
Filed by a wife made vindictive by the scandal
Of a bastard sired by her husband, with her sister.
My bargaining position is not one of strength.
I've been arrested by the magistrate
And a bastard born cannot be ignored.
But a man of business is one who can negotiate
And there is no doubt I can play on Maria's pride
To turn this minor annoyance to a gain.
Yes, it should be easy; pride makes dupes of us all.
The bastard and his flaming hair can't be hidden
But his sinful origin can be forgotten
By simply adding him to Maria's clan.
The petty fascinations that are Natividad
Mean that soon there will be new misadventures
To set the women's tongues wagging
And the men nodding sagely at the latest scandal
But each secretly wishing that he'd been the participant.
If I can play off Maria's foolish pride
I may even get all that is her hereditary due,
Land and all that it can yield.
And if my dear Maria decides to resist
I've but to shake the Vicar of Christ in her face
And watch as she cowers as her Catholic past
Rises from the graves of her Spanish ancestors
And terminates the desire to divorce.
I can swear allegiance to a Christian potentate
But still can't deny I was born and raised Anglican
And thanks to good king Henry, divorce isn't a path to hell.

I have a pawn with which to negotiate, the inheritance
Of Jose de los Santos Butron,
The result of Josefa's and my love.
If all my property is promised to Maria's children
She will comply and the bastard will soon be forgotten.

The Botanist

It was good indeed to meet this man from Caledonia
Sent around the world to gather plants for English gardens.
He has the tact and diplomacy for which the Scots are known.
And intense as only a Scot can be.
But he's immune to the petty complaints I daily endure
And can talk in my native tongue.
And good company when riding with the Compania Extranjera,
A comic assemblage, jokingly called a militia, whose design was
To keep the silly southern Californians where they belong, worshipping
Government at the expense of business.
And the stories he tells, of lands densely clothed,
Beyond the vision or eye or mind with trees the size of our
Gigantic red pines, a land inundated by heavy rain
And peopled by artistic Indians plying the waters
In their huge dugout canoes, trading, warring and
Taking slaves to do their domestic chores.

Success

My dreams are slowly coming to fruition.
The lumber I produce forms a vital part
Of the economy of this part of California.
Granted, the competition isn't much as few persevere
In any business venture being readily distracted
By parties or fandangos, or getting money to attend them.
Any success has come against daunting odds.
The simplest of machines are not available to me.
Water wheels, a dream as unattainable as God,
Steam engines, even further beyond the pale.
The awareness of these mechanical marvels does exist
But the means to bring them about is lacking.
Artisans and mechanics don't grace this idyllic world.
What use is elaborate artifice to these people
When this undemanding land offers all you need,
Food, housing, mates and, through the missions, a path to God.

Oh to have at my lumber mill
The simplest of machines driving the Industrial Revolution.
Then I'd not be at the mercy of Indians
Who in spite of Catholic conversion still see tricksters
Creating obstacles to a Christian working day.
Just now these Indians cower under blankets
Hiding from the spirits who, they claim,
Have inflamed their skin and reduced them
To little more that dark-skinned scratching machines.
To hear these natives whine you'd think they were the first
To draw a saw through a redwood log,
Or sweat in the bottom of a pit
Bathed in fragrant sawdust.
The work may be called cruel
But it's not so because of the effort they exert.
No its the mindless boredom of the job.

How my fortunes would expand
And my ambitions find their goal
If I could but entice men with a mind like mine
And create an energetic group
Of artisans, tradesmen and capitalists
So I can feed on them, and them on me,
So my expanding wealth will be beyond the mercy
Of lazy and superstitious Indians.

Perhaps my dreams will soon come to completion.
It's just a matter of time until this place
Is a part of the United States.
American warships have been in Monterey Bay
And Col. Fremont is ranging over the land
Making sure the natives remain disorganized
And incapable of mounting any sort of military act.
But his efforts aren't really necessary.
The stubborn independence of the natives
Assure any organization will self-destruct in weeks.
And I'm well placed among the Americans.
A secretary to the American administrator
Placed in Monterey with the raising of the flag.
(Sweet Maria didn't like it at all—
She strapped her students who called it pretty.)
In my now political position I've many things to do
Auction ships and goods, hell even hang miscreants.

But my path to an enhanced fortune
Has become paved in Indian gold
Found in creeks flowing from the mountains to the east.
It sits exposed to all for the simple taking
And miners are flocking there to make their fortune.
I want my share, but not by shovel, pan and rocker.
I'll let others retrieve the gold, and then trade for it,
Not with Europeans or Mexicans elbowing for space
But with the Indians who gather gold
Although they can't fathom the frenzy it incites
In each wave of invaders who arrive by ship or land.

So it will be beads and trinkets for the Indians
And gold for me. It's a barterer's paradise
Each getting something valued in his society.
I've been on one trading trip
And returned with wealth beyond my dreams.
So now I'm off again in search of more Indian gold,
Across the swamps of central California to the foothills
Of the Sierra accompanied by good Californians including
One of my sons. When I return the "good" Maria will
Be amazed at the wealth I've generated for our family.
Tomorrow morning we ascend the Fresno River to seek the
Encampment of Indians where there will be gold for all.

Epilogue

he story told above came to an end near the Fresno River,
Finished by a blow to the head of Guillermo Roberto Garner.
Where he died and now rests is known only to his God.

REQUIEM IM PACE.

Biography

The poems here have a natural theme which is consistent with my botanical background. My previous books have been botany texts and a book of photos and poetry. I'm a native Californian living in Vancouver, B. C., with my wife Ellie, and am retired from the University of British Columbia.